MW01503834

AN ENCHANTED JOURNEY

Poetry that speaks of a journey of
learning, of life and of love

LADY MELODY CLANCY

Published in the United States of America

Brilliant Books Literary
137 Forest Park Lane Thomasville
North Carolina 27360 USA

ISBN:
Paperback: 979-8-88945-300-0
Ebook: 979-8-88945-301-7
Hardback: 979-8-88945-302-4

FOREWORD

These works are presented to all who care to read and feel the passion and love; to experience the emotions, concealed and unspoken and know there are others who long to share and long to receive the love of another. Melody Clancy is a beautiful woman revealing herself through the lights and darks of passion and loneliness. She gives the impression of one who has been here in another life and time. Her works remind me of Romantic poets like Burns and Byron. The haunting, mystical qualities of the poet's thoughts are seductive and inviting, yet filled with the loneliness of love denied. I see a very complex woman, mystical, close to the earth and elements and immersed in the physical world of today. The intensity and expression allow you to 'feel her breath on your skin' and 'hear her heart beat'. The tragedy, of unfulfilled love and the sincerity of love offered, is moving and extracts empathy from your soul. Sharing makes the loneliness less isolating and the poems are submitted for interpretation and appreciation by all of those who know this path.

Most would not reveal this private and passionate insight into their heart, their soul. An expansion of her first book, "Remnants from Within", "An Enchanted Journey" is offered to help heal and fill the void that exists when love offered is not reciprocated. Lady Melody Clancy is a distinguished lifetime member of the International Society of Poets (ISP). She has been published since 1996.

Ordained, a minister in 1996, Lady Clancy is a Shaman and currently studying to become an acupuncturist based in Traditional Chinese Medicine.

Appreciatively,

Tom Hankins,
Counselor, friend, confidant

This book is dedicated to
        "The Knight of my Heart"....

He showed me that I could truly know love.
He provided me with inspiration, strength
        and the ability to feel once again.

My Dearest Knight...
    My Love...
        My Best Friend...
Thank you for all you are, and all that you have
given me.

My Darling Scott, may you someday know
the blessings and richness in your life,
That I have found by having you in mine.

SHMILY

ONTENTS

$\mathscr{P}$REFACE

Lady Melody Clancy is a Shaman, a healer, a teacher and a student. She journeys through life with an awareness and acceptance like no one else I know. She provides strength and understanding to others, even to her own detriment sometimes. She is one of the very few "true" people I know. Many of us would like to know who this "mystery man" is, for as long as I have known Melody, I have never seen such contentment or such anguish in her. She says... that she has been given a special gift in knowing him and having him in her life, because most people don't find or know their true mates. He has captivated her, he is her mate of this I have no doubt, but I wonder, does he know? Melody is on a journey through life, love, healing and spirituality.

She invites you all to read, enjoy, feel, cry and rejoice in the words written from her heart.

A long time friend...

$\mathcal{I}$NTRODUCTION

These poems were written during great times of trial and tribulation, some about insights gained and some from great times of joy and of sorrow, it is about falling in love, being in love, and knowing love, it speaks of special children and special people. There are certain poems written at different times in my life and the dedication to who it is written is on the page preceding the poem to that person.

The book's dedication, to that someone special in my life, begins the book, he is my soul mate and though we are together, we are yet apart.. My love for him will always flow free and unconstrained..

I have lost one love in my life, he was taken from this Earth after such a short time of being together, and through that loss I have learned the special value, truth and essence of true love, it is unconditional and one should never belittle it or take it for granted, one should never push it off to the side, or put off the being with that one person, for the time together is so short, even if it is a full lifetime. Such a special gift given should be cherished and seized and such a special person in our lives should be honored, thanked and shown always how very special they are to us. To find ones Soul Mate is a special gift from above, one not many people, get to experience or know.

So treasure the gift and in doing so, the person and your life will so much more enriched and alive. Cherish the good times and walk proudly together through the rough times, pride in knowing that you have each been blessed with a most precious gift..

The gift of love.

LIMBING

Climbing upon a tree so tall,
Some how you scaled the castle wall.
My Knight... My heart, can you see
How very much you mean to me?
Ageless through time we've come so far...
Always together,
Never far from each others heart,
Or touch you see...
Meant to be together are you and me.

NEW YEAR

I am a New Year
Unblemished... Untouched...

A New Year
365 days... Uninhibited... Fresh...
New ... Full of promise....
A time to let go of regrets and unfulfilled
Dreams...

I am a New Year
Use me wisely... Thoughtfully...
Trust your heart,
Trust your mind,
And you will find that together we can
combine...

Into a New Year
Full of Love...
Fulfilled dreams...
Unimaginable desires...

A New time...
From you... From within...

I am a New Year,
So let us begin.

 For You

Together we stand,
    United we fall...

Intertwined...
    Our bodies....
      Our minds...
        Our souls....

Moisture glistens softly on your skin...
    Lubricating the friction,
      As you are buried deep within.

Your chest hair tickles, caressing my skin...
    I want to nibble, yet where to begin?

Your lips, your neck - Where should I go?
    To suck on your tongue so very slow?
      To taste your skin, and the Essence within.

I want to pleasure you, to please you, to feel you
within...
    So when and where can I begin?

"*You are an important being...*
Look within yourself"

SENSUAL KISS

The sensuality of a kiss begins with thoughts amiss....

Thoughts of a tender touch...
    A gentle caress...

Watching a person's mouth as they speak,
    The way their lips move,
Their tongue,
    as it slips out to moisten their lips....
        Thoughts of how soft those lips are.

The desire to reach out,
    Run your finger gently across their bottom
lip, feeling the softness.

A strong yearning to taste those lips...
    As you sensually caress them with the tip of
your tongue...
        Lazily...
          Slowly...

Seeking entrance ...
    to the warm depths waiting.

The sense of excitement...

As your Lover parts their lips in acceptance,
    In anticipation of what is yet to come.
Molding their body to yours.

Hungrily you plunge your tongue into the
    warm, moist depths...
        Filling your body with desire, hunger...
        You explore... tease, arouse.

Using your tongue to probe,
    and caress each surface of that wonderful
    mouth...

Seeking the deepest recesses,
    Lost in the response your receiving...
Driven by the hunger that is building...

Tongue touching tongue,
    Body pressed against body...
Arousing...
    Warm and wet in the erotic dance of the
    sensual kiss.

Wanting more,
    yet not willing to leave this erotic dance...
This feeling that you will explode if you do
    not feed the urgency you feel building,

Then suddenly...
Surprised and startled...
   you feel a gentle tugging...
As your Lover begins to suck gently on your tongue...

You open your mouth further to hopeless abandon, as you are ...
   Awakened to the desire fulfilled...

   Only by the sensual kiss...

You & I

On a bed of roses we lay,
    Wrapped in a mysterious white haze,

Saturated by our passion for each other,
    In awe,
        For our souls have just touched...
        And joined...
Floating in a time that is neither here, nor there.

Like two hands forever intertwined,
    We are now tied together,
        By the silver cord that binds us all to our souls.

Ours,
    Yours and mine,
        Now twisted and joined,
            In both word and deed...

Our hearts,
    Our minds,
        Our bodies and our souls...
            Floating on an endless sea, together...

        Forever in Love.

I endure in order to reflect
Transcending order
I unite the matrix of endlessness
With the universal tone of presence
I am guided by the awareness and power of spirit

A Glass of Wine

A glass of wine and thoughts of you...
As I lay here exposed - what am I to do?

A glass of wine and thoughts of you...
I want your touch - I want to feel you...

A glass of wine and thoughts of you...
Your beautiful eyes and smile too...

A glass of wine and thoughts of you...
I Love you - I miss you - What more can I do?

"*Follow the rhythms of nature...*

Enjoy the beauty of the sunrise,
The peace and calm of the sunset."

HOPE

At the end of an exasperating day,
    I come to the waters shore.
        Where I sit mystified and spellbound,
          by the lure of the elemental cure.

The moon sits bright, ripe and full above,
    with a promise, of a coming love.

I close my eyes, I look and I see,
    There... your eyes looking back at me.

I listen to the sound,
    The song of the sea,
      I hear your voice
        A whisper,
          Calling out to me.

I stop and I think... how can this be?
    We are nothing more than friends,
      Friends... he and me.

My love runs deep, so strong and so true...
    I have fallen so deeply in love with you.

The waves so steady caressing the shore,
I sit and I ponder, what is yet in store?

The peace overwhelms me, taking me away
Giving me the strength to face yet another day...

The stars they twinkle and glisten above,
Reminding me in nature there is beauty and
love...

The majestic gray heron down by the sea,
Has come over to observe and give
acknowledgment to me.

I am once again renewed with hope,
in all that I see...
Knowing that hope,
Will once again sustain me...

Hope guides me through the day..
And especially the night, the hope that once you
are gone from my sight...
It will not be the last time,
that my heart will take flight.
That one day soon I will look upon you
and you will know...
How very deep the depths of my love for you go.

With all that I am and all that I possess...

I remain yours,
The Lady of your heart.

I harmonize in order to influence
Developing Wisdom
I unite the process of free will
With the Universal harmonic tone of integrity
I am guided by the power of potential

KNIGHT OF MY HEART

Knight of my Heart..
  Knight of my Dreams..

Only in passion does it seem we loose all of our
boundaries...
  We shed all our confinements.

Then we each touch our hearts, and there, together...
  It's true,
      we find ourselves united as it should be..

There and then do we each find peace..
  Wrapped in each other's glorious light..

We touch, we feel, we know the extreme,
  Then reality hits us and it seems like a dream.
    For time is short and you must go,
      And once again we must say goodbye.

IT'S NO WONDER

You entered my life like the colors of the sunrise,
bringing light, warmth, comfort and a deep sense of
peace and well being, warming me, nourishing me
and awakening things in me, I had hidden away...
Never again to stray.

You have entered my dreams
with the beautiful words
only the heart can speak, and with gentle caresses
and offered me hope.
You have given me quiet kisses and sweet secrets
that my heart hungered for.

It's no wonder
I have fallen in Love with you...

I'll hold your hand on sunny days, and
help you through those rainy ways.
And if you forget what tomorrow holds, I'll
show you the way so you can be bold.
I'll walk beside you each step of the way,
give you space when you ask or you say.
I'll even slip into your dreams, filling you
with warmth, love and peace from within.

AN ENCHANTED JOURNEY

I'll be your partner, in all that you'll share,
I'll give you hope when you don't care...
I'll write you poetry, that only
my heart can speak,
And likewise I'll listen when your heart speaks.
And my love, my friend, I'll give to you
A new list of life's rules that
will include, happiness
and many sunny days, full of
light, love and golden rays.

I'll always be there for you, giving
you light to guide your way..

You have given me a light,
I thought I would never know,
My soul mate, my brave, did you
think anyone would know?

You have allowed me to express words and
a side of me I thought I could never show,
And gave me the strength to let
everyone know, who I am and what I
could be, simply by being only me...

That my life has been touched
in such a special way..
The way you have touched mine...

It's no wonder,
I have fallen in love with you

I motivate in order to know
Bonding healing
I confirm the store of accomplishment
With the expressive tone of service
I am guided by the enchanting power of magic

ꙅOLITUDE

Solitude,
    Silence,
        Sanctuary...

Water,
    Waves,
Lapping, Caressing...

Wind,
    Whispers,
        Words...
Comfort...

Warmth,
    Strength,
Safety.

Arms surround me from behind,
    Filling me with warmth,
        Strength....
Making me feel safe and strong..

I rest my body against his,
Feeling him from head to toe....
Feeling his breath on my skin,
The warmth glides gently over my skin.

Is it my Silent Lover giving comfort and energy
To me,
Or is it the essence of myself that I touch and find?

AWAKENING PASSION

Passion building spiraling inside...
I feel the pressure of your lips
when I close my eyes...
The warmth of your touch,
the gentleness in your eyes,
Makes me wonder, what do you hide inside.

Will I get the chance to see what's in there?
Sensuality and passion, those are both very clear.

The gift of friendship I hope will be,
The bases of whatever it is that we see.

Old friends yet new, what can this be,
friends and lovers you and me?

As you lay on the couch, your legs across mine...
I looked in your eyes and what did I find,
A man so sensual, naked and true,
was that really you?
It was hard to speak you caught me off guard,
What can this be...
friends and lovers, you and me?

I want your touch, the caress of your hands...
To explore your body, and experience the man.

To drag my hair across your naked body and
see your response, to suck gently on your
sensual lips, to feel your tongue touch mine,
As they dance slowly together in time.

I'll suck gently on your tongue
to entice you, you see.
Have you ever had that done?
If not, how can that be?

Am I being too forward, please forgive me.

Covered in dew our bodies intertwined...
The naked length of your body against mine.
The warmth of you there, the strength that I see,
How comforting it is, to be just me.

No shields, no walls, and no pretensions you see...
Just honesty and truth, between you and me.

We can be friends or lovers you see,
Maybe both together,
What is it that you want from me?

FEELINGS

Passion returns with the
dawning of each new day
Feelings rising leave me in dismay
Something so old yet so new
tell me what am I to do....

The gentleness of a feeling
the wonder of a caress...
I feel like I am not my best

The sensuality of a kiss upon my lips
can ignite the passion and bring such bliss
Arms to hold me, so strong and true
Allowing me to feel so much more than I do
tell me what am I to do....

Battered and broken, old yet new
My body lives despite the dew
Given the chance to begin a new
tell me what am I to do....

Passion once again to the fore
as each day passes wanting more
so alive and so dead what more can be said.

WHAT CAN THIS BE

I stop and I think what can this be -
   Is there more than there should be between
you and me?

I think of you often, I think of you fair -
   I want to feel your hands everywhere...

The touch of your lips, the caress of your tongue,
   The gentleness of your spirit -
      You are such a special one.

Yet there is apprehension in both you and me,
   So much fear what can this be?
Is this just illusion? What do you see?

Or is it a joke, fun just to see...
   just how far you can go with me.

Or is there a flame hidden deep in the smoke....
   yearning to be nourished...
      ...yearning to be stroked.

$\mathcal{F}$ALLING

Falling deeper the dew is gone,
and fallen into a melancholy song.
Each time you leave, I miss you so,
the pain gets deeper each time you go...
Will you ever know, will you ever see,
just how deeply each aspect
touches and effects me.
You are a part of me and I a part of you,
this neither of us can deny...
So why oh why, must we always say Goodbye?

I withdraw into myself in order to survive
Attracting and enhancing instinct
I honor the essence of my life force
With the commitment, truth and love of purpose
I am strengthened and guided
by my own power doubled

UNTOUCHABLE LOVE

I saw my love for the first time from a distance,
And knew once again my purpose....
Felt my birth...
My emergence once again....

My universe grown cold thru time,
Now warms to his presence in my life.

I hear his voice, and it washes over me,
Caressing my skin...
Warming my soul.

Gently at first, I felt the sweet
strains of our union,
Now his passion surrounds me,
Embraces me...
Holding me in its rapture.

His presence brings my tired,
abandoned hope a new meaning...
Our hearts, beating as one,
Heat up my cold universe.
Our time purified by our kisses,
Our eternity healed.

LADY MELODY CLANCY

*Yet here I am whispering his
name in the darkness,
Hoping somehow that my words will reach him.
Does he remember touching me...
Does he remember my voice
Not over the phone,
But close enough to feel my breath on his skin.....*

*Having touched his Loving essence I
know I will truly never be alone,
Yet seeing him with another....
I know he will truly never know
the depth of my Love.*

For you see his Love is untouchable to me....

*"Do what needs to be done,
for the good of all..."*

Whirlwind

A whirlwind of passion...
    A whirlwind of love,
        Carried me in its maelstroms high above.

Letting me touch...
    Letting me see,
        That which would never be there for me.

Twice to be given, twice taken away..
    So much of me lost, what more can I say.

My heart was once whole, strong and true...
    Now lays in shards, on the floor,
What more can I do?

The pieces of my heart so broken...
    and shattered you see,
So small they fit thru the eye of a needle,
beyond repair, there's nothing left there for me.
The stonewalls erected are so cold and so true...
    Locked somewhere deep inside is my love for
you.

Knight of my heart, there's where you'll see
deep in the walls where it should be, my love and
hope for you and me...
Buried in the shards...
      Empty and forgotten... with me.

He holds the key, not even he can see...
      The loneliness and emptiness that reside in
me....

 Some People

Some people come into our lives,
  and touch us in ways they do not know.

Some people come into our lives,
  and leave a wake of tears as they say goodbye
and go.

Some people come into our lives,
  and stand quietly by our sides,
    giving us support and hope as we flow with
life's tides.

Some people come into our lives,
  the impact they have they'll never know,
    because it is beyond words, beyond feelings,
with their strength comes an inner glow.

And some people come into our lives,
  and touch us in ways they do not know,
    for when the time we share is over…..
There is an emptiness and an absence we will
never again show.

"Open your heart and soul ...
to Universal Love"

$\mathcal{I}$N BETWEEN

I sit at the beach –
    The smell of the salt air permeates my senses,
The water laps the shore...
Gently...
      Softly...
      Warmly...
Like a gentle caress.

Yet tonight there is no comfort in what I see,
    Only emptiness and Loneliness surround me.

You breached the walls I built strong and high – a
castle reinforced thru time.

Yet somehow you got through,
    There's something very special in you...

Yet here I sit naked and alone...
    feeling empty for letting go –

For letting someone in.

I thought you wanted in – to be there,
    Yet your actions are very contraire.

You need time,
    This I know, another woman maybe so...
You see she's better than me.

I'll be your friend...
    I'll be your lover...
        I'd love to even be both.

But I cannot be in-between,
    It's very cold...
        And so lonely...
            It hurts in this place to be.

My friendship you have,
    That's easy you see,
        And friends we will always be.

And if you want to be lovers –
    What a compliment to each other we would be.

Is it fear or disinterest that keeps you from me????

Touch Me

Touch me,
   Hold me...
      Can you hear my plea?
I am weak and vulnerable can you strengthen me?

I am cold and alone how can this be,
   You say you have feelings, special for me....

I am void and empty nobody wants me..

I try and I try and I give and I do....
   What more is there, I don't want to fight for you.

I am not enough that's obvious to see,
   Someone else knows the pleasure,
      I imagined between you and me.

STONE HEART

Wounded pride a hollow cry...
    Cold and hurt and lonely inside.

I try to understand, try to find a reason why...
    Instead I find only emptiness,
    Loneliness and blackness...
                No light.

How does one fly, when one cannot see?

How does one feel, when one has no peace?

How does one try when one no longer has a heart,
    Beating warm with love and caring, the kind
given right from the start?

How does one love,
        when one has grown cold ...

    When one only has a stone heart?

"*Honor all your relations,
and they will honor you*"

TEARS OF UNCERTAINTY

Tears of Uncertainty fill my eyes,
As my dormant passion begins to rise.

Peace I had found, alone to be...
I locked away the passion,
where even I couldn't see...

Then I looked up and saw you looking at me,
searching and wondering, looking to see,
a friend or a lover, maybe in me.

Your kiss was gentle, uncertain and true
old acquaintances meet again, you and me.

I thought of you again from time to time
My thoughts, a will of their own...
no reason or rhyme.

I saw you again, how could this be,
you had such an effect on me.

Where others had failed,
you looked through to see,
inside of the shell I had built around me.

LADY MELODY CLANCY

My passion buried so deep, ingrained and
    true was pushing me to think
      more often of you.

So here we are now lovers to see
    if trust and friendship can also be.
Each with our hurts old so they seemed,
    came to the surface like a bubbling stream.

To haunt me or help me which should it be?
    As passion rises once more can you see,
      only in time we will know what is to be.

Your full of surprises,
    each time something new,
      Do I look so wonderful to you??

Tears of uncertainty fill my eyes,
    as passion is no longer on the rise,
its come to the surface, so glorious and new...

But you are not here, so what should I do?

Tears of uncertainty flow freely from my
    Eyes as I have said goodbye,
      yet one more time..

AN ENCHANTED JOURNEY

As I look inside what do I see?

I realize the love comes from inside of me
    and what I've been waiting for,
        was inside all the time.

Yet how do I show you, for you this is also true?

Tears of Uncertainty,
    still flowing from my eyes...
As I begin to realize, that love is not
    Important, at least not to you...

Therefore you can truly never know and see,
    The special gift in life,
        you and I have been given you see...

The beauty of our love and what it can be,
The richness that would come for all to see...

What you crave so deeply yet cannot be,
    because you deny what has been given,
        and what it should be...

The peace that would last an eternity, simply by
putting things as they should be...

    And being together...
        Being you and me...

BEING ALIVE

Cold and Indifference hurts inside..
    but then again so does being alive.

So where is one to go,
    If you can't hold it in and can't let it show?

I've tried taking them to heart,
    Keeping them apart from the pain and hurt
of the past...

But always at last the past is back,
    And the hurt continues to stack....

So goodbye my friends I have taken my last fall...
    I'll stand forever alone, just so to stand tall.

So my friends...
    To hell with you all!

FLEETING

These opalescent drops that wash my eyes...
    are the last of my hope and strength and pride.

As they roll down my face,
    I feel the last emotions fleeting,
        leaving only emptiness - no more meeting.

Emptiness engulfs me,
    sweeping over my soul like a wave.

The silence overtakes me as I give in... and go vague.

Look at me now... New and improved...
    empty and void...

No more hope... no more strength...
    nothing to give.. living now in reality,
        only the motions are there.

I let go of it all - no more strength to care.

If I can't give, I can't take...
    If I can't take, I can't share...
        If I can't share, no one can be there...

So that's how now I'll be - Cold and Unaware...
In the last fleeting moments... As I let go of what's
there... Even the words become fleeting...

As I no longer care.

ALL AROUND

All around what to see,
the gifts that life has given me,
the gifts withheld,
yet how can this be?
So much given...
and withheld from me.

MY SON

He is the Sun that lights up the
Daytime Sky...

He is the Stars that fill the Sky
at night...

He is Purity, Trust, Friendship
and Unconditional Love...

He is one that makes Life so
Special and worth living,

He is my Son..

Sunset

The sun is setting across the sky..
    Hues of orange, pink and lavender fill my eyes.

Peace and love are truly abound,
    Yet for me... not to be found...

Hope resides so deep within...
    Will this loneliness come to an end?

When will I know...
      When will I see...
A smile...That is there, just for me.

Will I again ever know
    when I need it to be,
Someone is waiting there, just for me....

Tears fill my eyes as the setting sun dies...
    Turning the sky crimson...

Now darkness resides...

And Passion...
> *Once again, hauntingly now on the rise.*
> *Burns so deep, So deep inside.*

I toss,
> *I wonder,*
I tremble at night,
> *For when closing my eyes,*
> > *Safety and security take flight...*
Leaving me alone...
> *Naked and bare..*
> > *Will I ever know again the safety and*
comfort that's there...

Lost in his arms and love for me...
> *Will there ever be love again for me?*
There was one once... given so easy and free,
> *Circumstances took him so quickly for me.*

To walk by the shore hand and hand and to be...

> *Lost in the rapture of the sunset I see....*

I unify in order to share
Attracting knowledge and wisdom
I use the process of free will
With the energetic tone of purpose
I am guided by my intuition,
Power and strength doubled.

Thank You

The friendship you show,
    The Love that you shine is a beautiful gift
      to me and mine.....

Our relationship though we cannot define
    is something we know has come thru time,

Special times past and free...
    I'm glad that once again here and now we see.

Our paths have crossed and come to be...
    The most special gifts we have are free.

Thank you for being here in time,
    Thank you for loving me and mine.

So Alone

A Thousand images flowing by...
muddled feelings, why can't I cry...

Wanting to give...
    Needing to give...

Yet where to begin..
    so long since I've felt more than a press on the
skin.

These stonewalls,
    built so strong and so high...

That continue to grow...
    being reinforced each time,
        encasing my greatest treasure.

A heart made of stone so carefully carved
    I feel so alone...

Though I must be strong..
    for everyone you see,

Yet who will be there and be strong for me?

"*Take from the Earth
only what is needed...*

And nothing more..."

The next selection is for the two men,
physical therapists, who helped me
and taught me to walk again.
They helped me find the strength that
was still somewhere inside of me,
and lent me theirs when I
could not find my own...

For you Jason and Chris,
wherever you are...
Thank you.

THANK YOU FRIENDS

You gave selfless and unaware,
of the impact you would have because
you care.

Someone where strength could be found,
when inside there was no sound...

Someone who knew just what I needed,
to know it was OK to be just me...
pain and confusion there's so much
inside.

Yet thru your words and propriety,
you've helped me see...
there's so much more kept secretly...

Hidden away so only a few can see,
there's so much more than superficiality...

Thank you for being you,
Thank you helping me see,
there's so much more left inside of me.

HEALING WATER

Healing Water,
    caress me,
       touch me,
          and heal me...
Warm my heart and let me know,
    the gentleness of a caress.

I would like to experience the warmth of a
    touch, the sensuality of a feeling,
      The sincerity of a friend.

Fulfill in me that which no one else cares to.

I seek reassurance from you that there is at
    least one who will accept me for that I am,
      and who is not ashamed of me,
        and all that I am.

DREAM CATCHER

The Dream Catchers there,
    the past once again found,
Made of wood and feathers,
    my destiny wound.

The Dream Catchers here,
    Spiraling, spinning round...
Magick and mystery come forth and abound.

Caught in the web,
    Spiraling, spinning round...
Will my feet ever again touch the ground?

In the veil of the mysticism caught,
    Spiraling, spinning round...
Learning and growing, where am I bound?

In the Dream Catchers web,
    Spiraling, spinning round...
I live in the Shadows,
    My essence and I bound...
Will anyone care, reach up and pull me down?
For I am in the Dream Catchers web...
    Waiting, spiraling, spinning round.

"All Life is sacred, treat all beings with respect, including yourself."

Special Angels

Special little angels who come our way,
  Special little angels who help us get through
each day.

A gentle caress...
  A longing touch...
    Somehow they let us know they need us so
very much.

Some people say what do you do? I could not live
that way..

I look at them and say... why? I am so blessed
each day.
  For in my life, this special little one, is a special little angel...

My special little son...

STOLEN AWAY

When someone special,
    is stolen away from us,
The way to keep them alive is to love them.

Accidents happen, occurrences come and go,
    But true love never dies,
it travels through time and space,
    Journeying from place to place...

Until both souls can touch,
    and be in the same place..

United once again,
    whole and free..
Knowing the love,
    that only between them can be.

"Do nothing...

yet leave nothing undone"

RAGING STORM

I sat there on the beach,
the storm raged violently.

The waves pounded the shoreline
in angry thrusts,
As if trying to express all its emotions...

Confused and angry,
the waves continued to hit the shore.

The shore seemed to open up
and swallow each wave
In a silent promise of acceptance...

As I sat there on the beach,
the storm calmed,
And the waves began to caress the shore...
Gently...
Lovingly....
Thanking it for its acceptance.

I sat there and I watched the storm...

Drawn by some unknown force,

not able to leave... Only able to feel,
Because I too was angry and confused.

And as I watched the storm,
    I felt my anger dissipate...
Leaving only confusion and loneliness...
    Hoping one day someone will accept me,
        As the shore accepted the storm.

Left in awe by the beauty,
    The beauty of what I have just seen,
I realize the beauty and love to be found in life...
    And I feel comforted...
Taking the silent invitation,
    I walk to the shores edge,
Letting the water gently caress and love me,
    Washing away the loneliness and Confusion....

Feeling a sense of peace and love,
    Calmed by nature and it's beauty....
        I leave the beach...
My silent lover to face another storm....

$\mathcal{I}$LLUSIONARY $\mathcal{V}$EILS

Illusionary veils, encase and surround, they stand
through time, as each life goes round...

Protecting the person, encasing the heart
        To surround, the most precious of our treasures...
Deep within where they can't be found.

The soul... this is treasure, the fragments, the pieces..
        Scattered through time...

We don't miss these pieces
        until there comes that special time when a gift
is given, a gift from above...
        The purest of gifts, the gift of love...

Then we take back those fragments,
        and piece them anew
To create a new veil as each of us must do...

Though the question remains, the same for
        each time...
Is this veil real or another illusion....

                        I will loose again this time?

My Path

The path I am on is winding and strong,
The journey I seek is deep with in me.
The stones of my path I gather and craft,
To be what you see, it's the essence of me.
I walk and I wonder, I travel and I see....

What do I want the result to be?

Serenity and Harmony,
Peace, Balance and Hope.
The Love of another to help me cope,
to walk by my side, when needed my guide.
To whom I can give all that you see....

Someone to share the essence of me.

THE ESSENCE OF ONE

She stood bright and tall,
 In the background a flowing waterfall.
The crystal blue water, tears, flow from her eyes...
 Forming a pool at her feet,
Then the river where the falls do meet.

She stands alone, but never free,
 Giving to those who come in need...
Words of wisdom or a comforting touch,
 The ability to give, she has so much....

Take a look when the moon is full,
 If you open your heart you will see....
The glimmer of a horn pure gold....
 Feel the touch of a soul untold..
 And know the essence of her, she who will be,
Alone forever...
 Yet how can this be?

CHILDS THOUGHTS

Here now it's time to see...
In school studying what can I be??

It seems endless the work,
*   How can this be?*

No time to play,
*   What are they doing to me?*

Using my time for things I just don't see.

A fireman, a policeman, how hard can that be?
*   Why do I have to work so hard to be an aver-*
age person?
Simply just me...

Because I am more than average, more than I yet
see..
*   So I'll learn and study to be the best I can be.*

DEEP MIST

Longing to be touched..
   stroked and caressed, what to do?

To know one is someone to be needed and
   missed, to know one has value
      amongst the deep mist.

To be touched so gently to test and to see...
   If one can still feel....
Is it just pressure on the skin or deeper
   and meant just for me...

This is the trade that I make, to be all that I can
be... To give to others so they can learn
   and be better at being.

I feel so different cold and calloused,
   yet know to be true, a pillar of strength,
      if they only knew.

I bury my needs and wants too deep to be seen, I go
forward and move on so that no one will know...
Just how deeply in the mists...
   the seeds are buried beneath the snow.

Setting Sun

Whispers upon the ocean I see,
  The sun is setting are you thinking of me?

The orange and gray hues as the sun subdues,
  bring the loneliness again to the fore...

The sun is setting upon the beach,
  I have been here so many times before,
    I whisper your name alone... once more.

Now only an ellipse remains,
  as the essence of my hope once again drains.

Once again to the fore,
  the loneliness envelops me and burns to my
core.

This next selection is to a very special person in my life, not only has she been my teacher is Western Sciences in school, she has been a strength and support to me through my education and life at this time in my journey. She is a friend and one of the very special gifts that came out of an event that has transformed my life. Thank you Dr. Catherine Cover for your love, your strength and your patience.

My Teacher, My Friend

*I know this special person you see, She has
become a dear friend and support to me...
She is full of such incredible love you see...
She makes me feel special and
she doesn't even know,
For when I look at her , I see an inner glow...
The knowledge she holds, I wish I could know,
One benefit of her love is she helps me grow, the
support and gifts you give are priceless you see...
Thank you for being such a special gift to me.*

"THE ONES..."

Transindental life as one flows through time,
Making decisions,
Determining the out come,
Then wondering why...
As one goes through the "occurrences"
of the decisions one made,
One wonders why?
Why does one "suffer" the discomfort?
The discomfort of the conflicting emotions,
Until the result or the decision manifests...
And the union is made.
To learn? To learn what?
Lessons still to be had? For there are many,
Or is it the lesson that,
Thought one knows love is the purest of all,
One does not trust the truth - the essence..
So therefore,
One must learn to trust in the contradictions,
And look beyond them.....

"We often miss the opportunity,
and in doing so miss life...

And in missing life,
miss the why and who we are...

and what we are..."

For Peace

A poem for peace for all to see...
A poem to bring happiness,
compassion and serenity.

Some go through each day,
some go through each night,
Enchanting spells to engulf all
in a glorious light.

Each of us wondering how,
how we could bring about such a plight?

It boils down to each one,
Each on of us you see...
Each one of us working towards such peace,
Each of us aware of the humanity,
Each of us aware there is such a need.

So I'll go through each day,
I'll go through each night, enchanting
spells to bring about such a plight.
Sending love and hope to those in need,
For all they have to do is ask and it shall
received, such is the gift of Reiki, to all,
to all who are in need.

A PRAYER

I stand clean and strong..
In the pale moonlight,
My hands raised,
my fingertips touching the velvet
and starry night.

The salt water of the sea,
caresses me, the ebb and tide
Pulling gently at my feet.

The moonlight, softly shining...
The glow a reflection,
softly whispering my passion...
Winds.. Carry my wish, carry it...
Now go!

Come to me My Lord, My Light,
Come to me in this darkness of night.
I'll cherish your gentle tenderness,
Guide you into the light.

I pray to the Goddess, I pray to the God...
Come to me, come bathe in our passions
bright glowing fire.

My Lord, embrace me,
Within the loving warmth of your arms.

We share a timeless burning flame...
Our place together we are now to claim.

Enchantress, Lady of the Moon,
Hunter Lord of the Sun,
Help me, my soul is lost within his eyes...

Come to me My Lord,
We will dance the dance of eternal love...

Wrapped in our passion carried
on our flowing desires...

Caress my lips with yours,
Leave them wet and quivering...
Yet once more.

Grace be the sea, the moon my guiding light,
My Lord is lost in darkness,
I am no longer his light.

My Lady, My Lord...
This burden is heavy,
The weight too much to bear...

How do I close my heart to love...
A love that has transcended time.

LADY MELODY CLANCY

How do I shield my heart from love,
A truth, I thought was there...

How do I close my heart to love...
A love so distant, yet there...

ORN

I sit amidst a gently lit dining room, the lights soft white and candle light. The soft glow envelopes me as I relax, as I drift back in time. As I look out the full "wall" window, there is an oak tree, old, beautiful and draped in moss, overlooking a lake, the water still and unhurried...

As the sun has just set and I look again out the window the candle light is reflected in the glass, it looks like fairies dancing in the moss of the tree, peeking out and smiling - saying hey, here look at me.

The lights across the lake now have reflections on the water, like fingers inviting me into their depths, offering healing and cleansing. The atmosphere outside is serene and quaint, surrounded by orange groves and wild jasmine, the smell is intoxicating, the atmosphere and the "feeling" are romantic, soft and peaceful.

My room is small, clean and charming, no distractions, just a special place for two to be - but alas I am here alone, with only myself to face and be with, and I feel... not emptiness... for my life is rich you see, but very alone... for there is no one to share the "beauty" and peace that surround me.

The wine I am drinking intoxicates me, opening me, dropping the barriers and the walls, relaxing me - yet I am torn... ...For there is no one to share the warmth that emanates from me, no one to share the love that flows free and easy from me.

I close my eyes and I see your beautiful blue eyes, smiling at me, and tears come to my eyes...

I take a deep breath and go further into what I see, I feel the warmth of your body, feel the "completeness" we both feel as our bare chests brush against each other...

I can feel the comfort and passion that overwhelms each of us, as we relish in the few moments we find in time - and again I am torn ...

*... Comforted by the few moments in time we
do get, and saddened knowing once again I will
climb into bed and it will be empty and cold ...
... knowing you are somewhere else, laying next
to someone else, feeling the warmth of their body
and not mine ... knowing that is your choice to
be there and not with me... and I am torn...
... I don't just hear your words of
feelings towards me but "feel" the
connection that has come thru time with
us – that is so strong now, still ...*

*Something nudges my arm,
and as I look to see I am staring
straight into the eyes of the wolf,
your eyes, as if to say I AM HERE!...*

*I am with you and again I am torn...
... for though he lays at my feet, and I can
"touch" the energy, there is no warmth,
the essence is there and with it comes a
certain comfort, and again I am torn...
... for is this all I am allowed..*

*This is the wolf's first appearance to
me since this journey began and I am
comforted by his, your presence, I feel
"safe" because he, you are with me..
Yet I am alone..*

*The tears flow freely now, and the
wolf sits up, his paw upon my leg..
his, your eyes boring into mine..
... A silent plea ...
And in my heart there is no question...
For I always want you with me...*

... and I am torn...

MEMORIES

There is beauty in memories,
Comfort in wisdom gained,
But hope....
How does one find hope?

Hope that what and who they,
are means something...

Hope that what they do counts..

And hope that one day...
The beauty....
The comfort...
And the hope will converge...

And there will be peace and love?

TIME IS FLEETING

Time is fleeting, Time has past,
   and still my lover..
      Our love he cast..
The days they pass..
Lost in daily grind, unfelt and unknown..
Myself, a silent voice who's heart is unknown.

The shadows grow tall,
   the leaves wither and die...
And the soul closes tightly like the rose bud ..
   Carved in stone, closed and eclipsed.
Like myself, a silent voice who's heart is unknown..

Never again to know the love of another...
   For my commitments to my mate,
      stand strong and true...
And though he acknowledges all that we are...
   He chooses to go thru the days,
      And the nights as you see..
Next to another, one who is not me.

   So what is left, what can be? ...
      For the Universe has forsaken me..

WISHING

As I look out at the star lit sky,
I wonder have you thought of you and I?

I only wish that you could see,
Just how much you mean to me.

I wish I was laying next to you each night,
As we each look at the heavens,
the stars so beautiful and bright.

Our passion, our love what is to be?
I only wish that I could see..

As I look at the stars, I am wishing you see..
and I am wondering..
Are you thinking of me?
And together how wonderful we would be?

I LONG

I long to feel his soft furry body,
  naked next to mine...

I long to feel his warmth,
  as I am wrapped in his arms...

I long to feel his breath,
  as it caresses my skin in soft whispers...

I long to feel his lips,
  as they softly caress mine...

I long to smell his scent as our breaths mingle together,
  in words of passion and love...

I long to feel safe,
  knowing he is asleep next to me...

I long for you Scott,
  And all that we are together...

  Even when we are apart...

HOPE AND DESPAIR

Hope and despair are not opposites,
They are cut from the same cloth,
Produced from the same circumstances,
Created from the same mold.

Hope is not based on the ability
To create a better future,
It is founded in ones ability to look
With a new understanding at a difficult past
or challenging experiences.

The fact is, that the memories
or experiences we have learned from,
Are the basis or seeds of our hope.

If those experiences continue to
be negative for too long,
In spite of applying what we have
learned from the past,
and viewing things from a
different understanding,
then we lose hope...

Hope is not some kind of fantasy world
to be resorted to
because we simply cannot face the hard facts
that threaten to swamp our hearts.

The wrong choices are sometimes made,
Evil does exist, yet we make
those choices, do we not?
For every event in our life is a choice
we make, and we can change those
choices, learn from them,
And make them better experiences.

Even through it all, hope remains, or does it?

As with all things hope is a choice,
A choice we base on the seeds planted
from past experiences and memories.

Hope is a choice based on love,
Love we do see or feel despite all else,
and for the human soul,
That is the love of another...

So how does one turn to hope,
When they do not have the love of another??

AN ENCHANTED JOURNEY

The difference between Hope and despair
Is that despair,
shapes an attitude of the mind,
Hope creates a quality that becomes
an essential part of ones soul.

So where does one turn when they have
exhausted and can no longer find that
quality of hope within themselves?

Life is not one road, but many,
and sometimes we take the wrong road,
This does not leave us stuck
for it is simply a choice we have made
and we can change that road,
Simply by choosing a different road,
or making a different choice.
The traveling of the different roads,
Changing the choices in our lives,
Provide us with the basic material
within which
we find hope in the midst of despair.

It is within this hope found,
that we are carried through,
and beyond the dark night of despair...

To the dawn of new
and different understanding...

LADY MELODY CLANCY

A new sense of strength and a new wisdom
that has been planted in,
and becomes an essential part of our soul.

Yet I continue to ask...

Where does one go...

When they feel
they have exhausted their hope,
And they have not the love of another?

A SPECIAL MAN ... AND A SPRINGTIME BREEZE

You came into my life,
   on a springtime breeze...
A simple kiss at a wedding of some friends,
   is how it happened you see.

Time went past and still we resisted to be,
   for work stood in the way,
      Yet we saw each other each day.

I helped you through some pretty troubled
   times you see...
It seemed a friend you had found in me.

A little gift here, a little gift there...

It was a way to share, to know of the other,
   though they couldn't be there.
Strawberries were your favorite, I believe...

Soon it became overwhelming and we
    decided to see,
What could there be between you and me?

Two beautiful girls,
    I would have gained you see...
Quite a family we would have had,
    you and me
        I think of them still ...

So soon you were taken away from me,
    So much more we were yet to be.

I held your hand as you breathed your last...
    I told you I loved you just as you passed.

    Simple words, we are all so afraid to say...

We don't know what we've had,
    until the persons gone away.

Yet things happen for a reason,
    though we do not always see...
A few years later,
    a special gift you helped me see...

"Give constant thanks...
to the Universe,
for each new day..."

"A fearful defense...
can never defend...

IRCLES

Round and round and round it goes,
and where it stops nobody knows...

You are the one that knows,
You can stop it and see,
And start a new process of what you can be,
What you can have,
and what you can know...

It starts with a beginning, a letting go...

Let go of the things
that are not pleasant to be...
Let go of the things
that hurt and you will see...

A new beginning as things begin to shift...

A new beginning, as you make a new rift...

LADY MELODY CLANCY

A new and different consciousness,
A light to guide the way,
The strength and courage
to follow your heart,
As you go about your way...

No more walking round in circles,
Trying to find your way,
But rejoicing instead
because you found a way,
To follow your heart,
And live your life your own way...

Now it is all much clearer
and brighter you see,
Because you can live without fear,
and be who **YOU** *want to be...*

I harmonize in order to transform
Modeling energy
I unite the environment of self-generation
With the universal tone of integrity
I am guided by the power of abundance

OUR PATH

Our paths have met we walk as one
Nature calls us into the sun

We walk gentle and soft each step new
We ask the questions we learn life's truths
And know our love together will be bright

Our journey continues, roads twist and turn
But deep in our hearts love's fire will always
Burn for one another deep and true

"Speak the truth,
but only in the good...
not bad in others."

That night and each night since...
I have truly walked alone...

For fate has left me adrift,
without so much as a wind...

To carry him to the
shores of my love.

I retreat into my inner essence...
To align with the transformative
energies of nature.
I open my heart and mind to the
wisdom that surrounds me.
I overlook the entrapments and
obstacles to see the truth.
I am empowered by the essence of
the truth and live in its wisdom.
I gain knowledge and strength
from unifying myself
with the essence of truth ...
I empower others through this wisdom to
Find their essence of truth and love.

NOUGH

I love you enough to stand by your side.

*I love you so much I will work
through the difficult times.*

*I love you enough to give you the space you need
And not burden you with my stuff.*

*I love you enough to desire you night and
day not just physically but all that you are.*

*I love you enough to try to understand...
Even the pain and confusion.*

*I love you enough to help when I can...
Let you be when I can't, yet be there still.*

*I love you so much that I ache...
For you...
For us...*

I love you enough to see that this love...
Our love...
May not be enough for you...
So and My lord...
My love...

I love you enough...

...to let you go...

A MESSAGE TO MY LORD...

Just when I've thought this out, and concluded that these feelings I have for you are pointless and make no sense and have resolved to turn them off, I find my desire and love for you overwhelming me, ruling against my determination, making me aware of the completeness that exists when we are together. Opening me to the feeling of peace that comes when we are together or in just knowing you are thinking of and wanting to be with me.

And then my whole body aches for you again, yearning for a touch I've never had, a pleasure I have yet tasted. Then, once again I'm unsteady on my feet, wondering will we ever know the happiness we find in each other, the joy of feeling each other through the night, the passion of waking in each other's arms, the joy in just knowing the other is there, and I sometimes find the common joys of life dull and empty.

And so, for good or for bad, I've decided to stop shouting accusations at myself and arguing with the Universe and simply accept that though I may never know, the joys mentioned above, that I love you heart and soul, that I can't change that, for it is as old and true as time..

I am yours until the end of time.. Centuries have come and centuries have gone and still here we are, together.. Yet apart...

You are in my thoughts..

I strive to perfect in order to nurture
Planting seeds
Sealing the input of emergence
With the Universal Harmonic
tone of manifestation
I am guided by the power
of Universal water

OPEN

As darkness comes into our lives, the mirrors of ones spirit reflect different journeys and paths yet to be taken. This is a time when our world changes and ones being begins to radiate, vibrate and glow.

Contemplate the new journey that has been on the periphery of your consciousness, it is an idea that has been nagging you. It seeks and awaits your invitation, to be planted within you to begin life.

The essence of your creativity will come after you begin the work on the sacred tapestry that is your life. It is then that the seeds of inspiration will begin to grow and surround you with warmth and cheer you on to growth and clarification.

Take responsibility for your actions, your work and your life and growth and manifestation will follow.

Take the journey and begin the liberation of your spirit. Feel the warmth of the glow around your body it is the astral field of energy that surrounds us all.

Feel the energy centers, the chakras, that sit like flower buds inside of the magnificent vase that is your physical body, as these buds open and bloom so blossoms enlightenment of the spirit.

Closing Thoughts

We all through ignorance have misused the power bestowed upon us, at some point in our lives we come to a time when we choose to open and grow on a different level.

This level or opening may contradict our previous teachings or events in life, and if in these contradictions we are able to be open, one will find that our power can be restored, that universal spiritual law can help us be united again with prosperity, and that truth, though we may have separated ourselves from it, is and has always been there, it has never left us. It only waits for us to open again and realize its constant presence.

When we recognize the presence of love, truth and resonate with the awakening taking place within our spirits and accept these things in our life, they become abundant in our lives and we begin to live in peace and harmony, not only with our physical self but our spiritual selves, whatever that path may be for each of us.

Be in peace and love and unify all aspects of who you are into the wonderful being...

...you already are...

Know that all understanding begins with love and respect. The process begins with respect for The Great Spirit and time. All things and I mean all things have their own will and their own way and their own purpose...

...**This** is what is to be respected.

What is this will and time that it has the power to change all? What is this unseen force that is like the wind and can shape and change the land and our lives?

Learn to respect and to play with time...
                                    ...Time itself is surreal.

A person of power knows how to arrange time...
    Be aware of the time at which you do everything... ... and what you do.

Watch the transit of the stars...
Watch the moon awaken each night and the rising and setting of the sun, be aware of your cycles. Today's society is obsessed with time, so... now become time.

If you are obsessed with something, it is better to explore it than deny it. Then it is possible to give up the obsession and let a concept like time take its proper place in your life...

...Your power...
Depends on the use of time and respect.

"Enjoy life's journey,
But leave no tracks...

Printed in the USA
CPSIA information can be obtained
at www.ICGtesting.com
LVHW060410200923
758630LV00001B/6

9 798889 453024